# THE HUMAN BODY IN 3D

# THE STOMACH IN 3D

rosen publishing's
rosen central®

MAYA BAYDEN AND
JAMES TORIELLO

Published in 2016 by The Rosen Publishing Group, Inc.
29 East 21st Street, New York, NY 10010

First Edition

**Library of Congress Cataloging-in-Publication Data**

Bayden, Maya.
The stomach in 3D/Maya Bayden and James Toriello.
    pages cm.—(The human body in 3D)
Includes bibliographical references and index.
ISBN 978-1-4994-3613-6 (library bound)—ISBN 978-1-4994-3615-0 (pbk.)—
ISBN 978-1-4994-3616-7 (6-pack)
1. Abdomen—Juvenile literature. 2. Stomach—Juvenile literature. 3. Intestines—Juvenile literature.
I. Toriello, James. II. Title.
QM543.B39 2016
611.95—dc23

2015000143

*Manufactured in the United States of America*

# CONTENTS

# INTRODUCTION

Butterflies in your stomach? Have a gut feeling? These expressions aren't meant to be taken literally, but they do shed some light on the importance that we give to our stomachs. In addition to its anatomically central location in the body, the stomach also plays a central role in our day-to-day lives. Gut feelings aren't just an intuitive response; they're also what we feel every time we're hungry or eat something that maybe we shouldn't have. But there's more to the digestive system than just the stomach. Our bodies are well-designed machines, and the interconnected organs of the digestive system span from our mouths, where we insert food, to the colon, the last stop before waste is expelled.

Every time that a human being eats something, he or she is putting nutrition into his or her body. Imagine the last time that you picked something up from the supermarket. Whether it was a box of cereal or a candy bar, it probably had a label on the back with various nutrition facts. In their raw form, however, the body can't derive much benefit from these foods. In order to access nutrients listed on the back label, the body must first process foods. Digestion is the name for the process by which a series of organs in the body takes food and breaks it down into smaller substances, ones that the body can absorb more easily or expel as needed.

*A series of organs work together like a well-designed machine to carry out digestion in our bodies—converting food into the nutrients that our bodies absorb and the waste that it expels.*

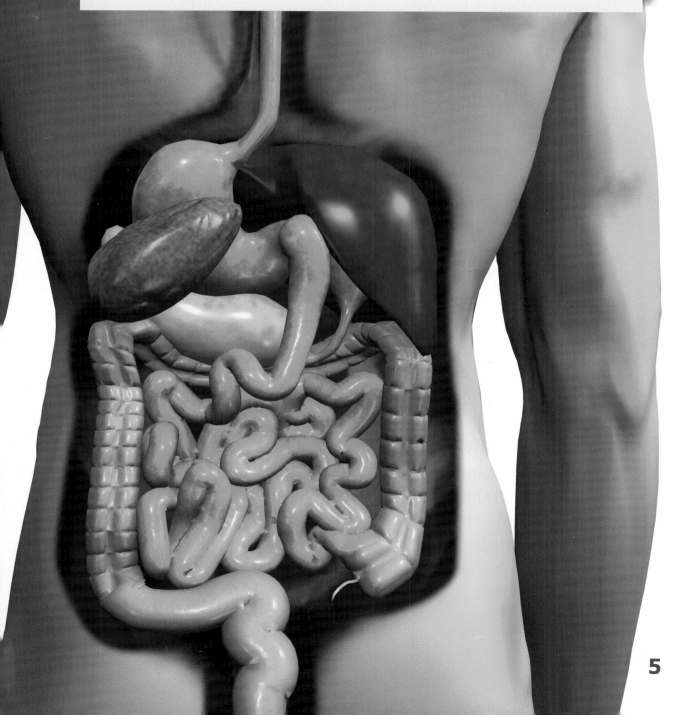

The digestive process begins with something as simple as our teeth and saliva. When we chew our food, we're physically breaking it down into a small enough form for it to be able to pass down through the esophagus—the path to the stomach. The stomach plays a key role in chemically digesting proteins in our food. After the stomach, the remaining substance passes through both the small and large intestines, where further nutrients are absorbed into the bloodstream. Whatever the body can't use continues on to the colon before being eliminated as waste.

The process might sound fairly straightforward, but in reality there is a complex series of physical and chemical processes that occur in a number of different organs, all for the sake of helping the body get the most out of the foods we consume. In addition to the important organs mentioned above, the liver, gallbladder, pancreas, spleen, and kidneys also play essential roles in helping break down food, absorb nutrients, and eliminate waste from the body. If any of these organs didn't perform its job, there could be serious health consequences for a person trying to digest food.

Here, we'll take an in-depth look at each of the organs involved in the human digestive process and its unique task in our body's machine. Furthermore, all the exciting action is illustrated with photo-realistic 3D renderings of the various organs and, in particular, the stomach. These accurate images give us a peek into the inner workings of our complex digestive machine and all the nuts and bolts that make it churn. So if you think you can stomach the real details about the digestive process, then get ready for a better view than you've ever seen before.

# CHAPTER ONE

# IT'S CRUNCH TIME: BEHIND THE ABS

Belly, stomach, or tummy—these are the most common terms that we use when we complain about a pain in our midsection. But our midsection, or abdomen, actually contains many other vital organs besides the stomach. The midsection houses almost the entire digestive system, our body's food factory and energy distribution center. The abdomen, or trunk, also contains powerful muscles and important bones. These connect the upper and lower body and provide a safe place for digestion to take place.

Like other areas of the body, the abdomen also includes blood vessels, which ferry nutrients to needy cells and organs. The nerves in the trunk communicate sensations to the brain and send directions to muscles. And the lymph vessels help fight bodily intruders, an important consideration for the digestive organs.

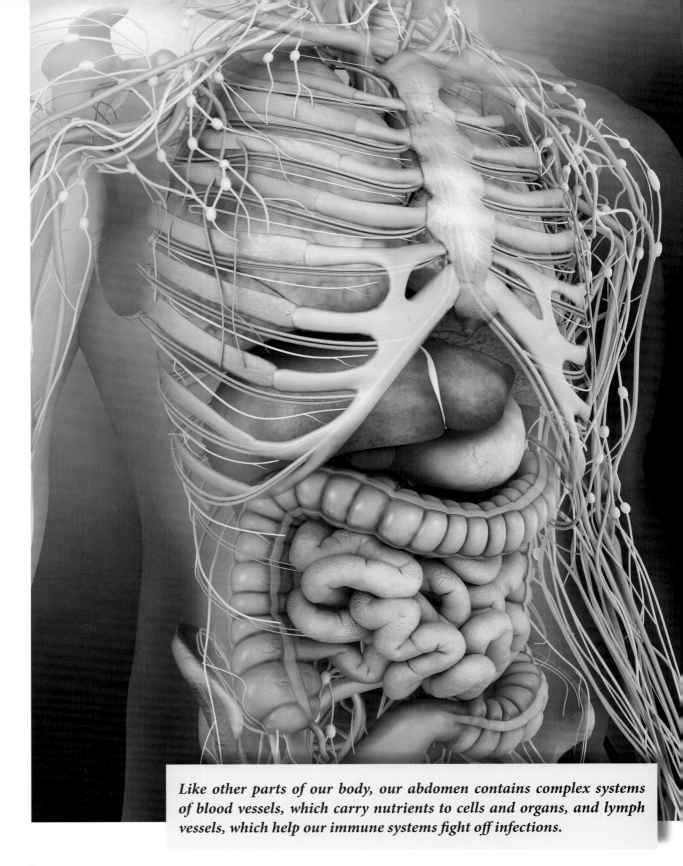

*Like other parts of our body, our abdomen contains complex systems of blood vessels, which carry nutrients to cells and organs, and lymph vessels, which help our immune systems fight off infections.*

# OUR ABDOMINAL MUSCLES

As in other parts of the body, the skin of the body's midsection covers a layer of fat. There are two parts to this layer. The outer layer can be thick or thin, depending on a person's weight. In fact, this is the part most of us pinch when we're trying to see if we're fat or not.

The outer layer of fat is known as Camper's fascia. *Fascia* is a Latin word meaning "bandage" or "girdle." It is used in anatomy and medicine to describe body tissues that bind structures together. Camper is the name of an early Dutch physician and scientist named Pieter Camper, who lived in the eighteenth century. Today, Camper is best known for discovering that birds' bones have air spaces in them.

Body builders are often admired for their shapely abdominal muscles. The shape comes from a number

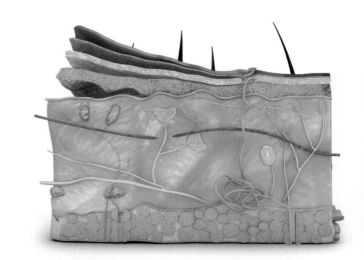

*Underneath the skin of our abdomens is a two-part layer of fat. The outer layer of fat, called Camper's fascia, may vary in thickness from person to person. It keeps us warm and protects the abdominal muscles, which are beneath it.*

of interwoven muscles. They're not just for show; they give the abdomen flexibility and help to protect and hold the interior organs together. They also assist the diaphragm during breathing and help in the body's elimination of waste. When women give birth, the abdominal muscles help push the baby into the world.

Five main muscles make up the abdominal wall. Three are flat. They compress and support the trunk of the body. They run almost like bandages wrapped in slightly different directions around the midsection. They are the external oblique, internal oblique, and traverse abdominal muscles. A mirror image of each muscle extends around each side to the center of the body. These halves lace together at the linea alba, Latin for "white line," which is what the thick sheet of tendons at the end of the muscles looks like.

## IT'S ALL GREEK TO ME

Many anatomical terms come from Latin and Greek words. There are many reasons for this. Western medicine dates to Greek and Roman times. Latin was the common language in Europe during the Roman Empire. Doctors naturally spoke it and used it to describe body parts as well as medical concepts. After the fall of Rome, Latin remained a common language of learning. Students and teachers used it to communicate with each other even if they came from different places. Their texts were also written in Latin. Since the human body hasn't changed during historical time, there was no real need to invent new names.

The linea alba contains small blood vessels and nerves that run out to the skin. It also has an unusual hole—the belly button. This is all that remains of the umbilical cord that connected the developing fetus to its mother before birth.

The external oblique is the largest of the three muscles. Its fibers mostly run at a diagonal from back to front, or "inferomedially," as students of anatomy say. If you place your hands in your pants pockets with your thumbs sticking out, the direction of your fingers will be in roughly the same direction as the muscle fibers. The internal oblique muscles form the next layer, fanning out from about the hip. The transverse muscles form the inner layer. These go around the midsection.

The rectus abdominis and pyramidalis muscles are vertical muscles. They help flex the trunk of the body. If you've ever done a sit-up or even just bent over, you were putting them to work.

Three or more sections of the rectus abdominis line up in pairs down the front of the body. These sections are connected by thick tendons. When a body builder tenses these muscles, the stomach seems to bulge with a series of ripples or steps. The overall shape is often compared to a washboard.

Surprisingly, twenty percent of humans do not have the pyramidalis, a small triangular muscle near the pubic area at the base of the rectus abdominis. This muscle tenses the linea alba at the very bottom of the abdominal wall.

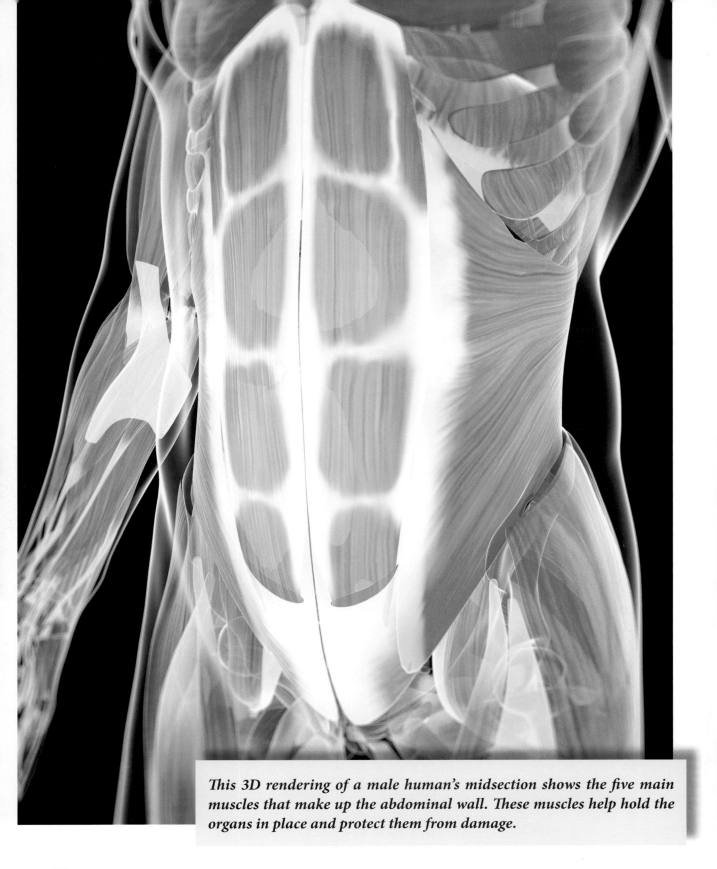

This 3D rendering of a male human's midsection shows the five main muscles that make up the abdominal wall. These muscles help hold the organs in place and protect them from damage.

# THE BONES IN OUR MIDSECTIONS

Below the skin and muscles, bones shape the body. The lower ribs and pelvic bones cradle the midsection. The backbone, also known as the vertebral column, joins them together.

The vertebral column protects the spinal cord and spinal nerves, which are like telephone or computer wires connecting the brain with the rest of the body. The spine also helps support and balance a person as he or she stands, sits, and moves. Overall, there are thirty-three vertebrae, or small bones joined by discs, in the spinal column.

The vertebrae interlock like the pieces of a small key chain. Bony wings face the

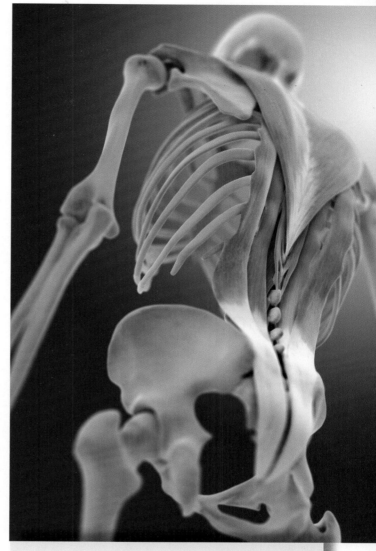

*The skin and muscles aren't the only body parts that hold our organs in place and protect them. Our skeletal system is made up of a network of bones—including the ribs, pelvic bones, and vertebral column—that help protect our other bodily systems. It also provides balance and support.*

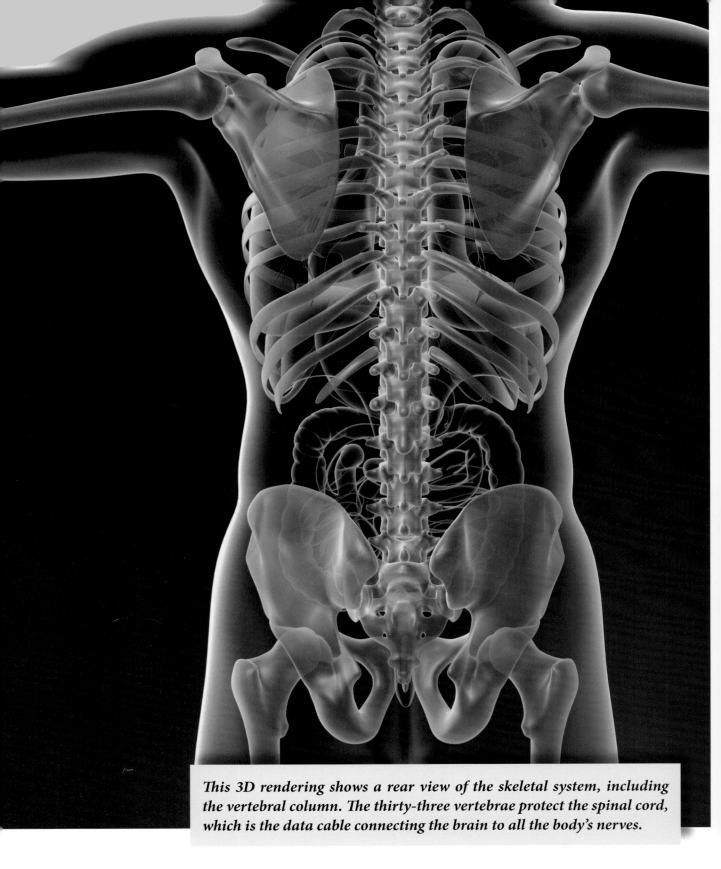

*This 3D rendering shows a rear view of the skeletal system, including the vertebral column. The thirty-three vertebrae protect the spinal cord, which is the data cable connecting the brain to all the body's nerves.*

back and sides of the body. The discs between the bones work like tiny rubber washers between these connections, giving the back some flexibility. Muscles along the column add strength and stability.

Rib bones fan out from the spinal column to the front of the body. Without skin, muscle, and internal organs, the ribs look a little like a birdcage or the framework of an unfinished building. This cage encloses the chest and abdomen, shaping the body and protecting the internal organs.

The ribs veer upward in the front of the body, forming a V on each side. This leaves the stomach and other internal organs room to expand in the front of the body. Every time you have a big meal, you take advantage of this space. It also gives surgeons easy access if they have to operate there.

The pelvis forms the base of the body's midsection. This strong collection of bones transfers weight from the upper body to the legs. Four bones do the job here, the two hip bones, the sacrum, and the coccyx. These bony structures are slightly different in men and women. In general, women's pelvic bones provide a wide opening to be used for birth. Male or female, the pelvic cavity contains the bladder, the rectum, and the genital organs.

# OUR INNER ORGANS

The body's digestive organs are often described as a long tube. That's a good way to portray the main part of the digestive

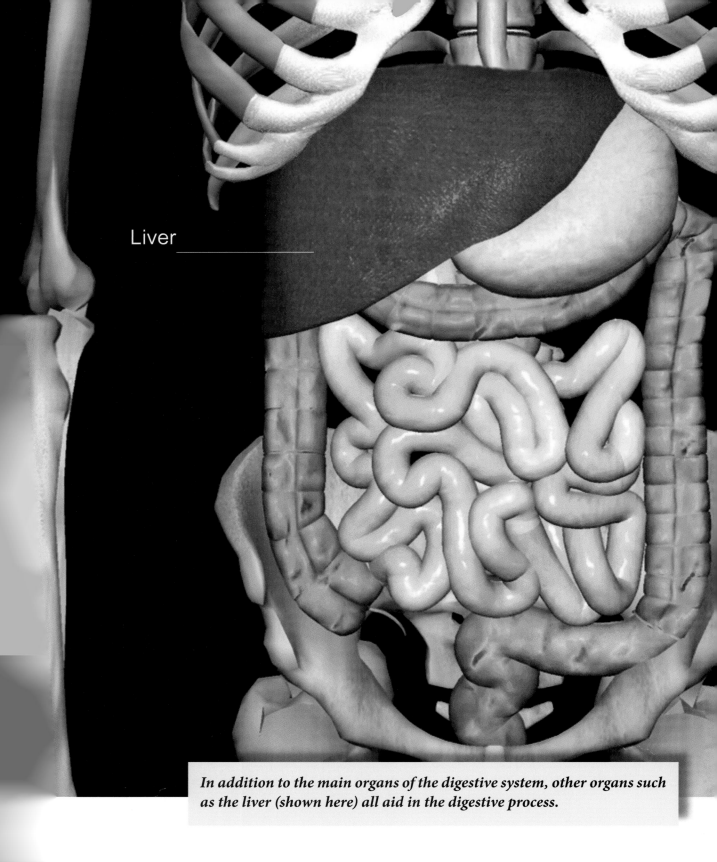

Liver

*In addition to the main organs of the digestive system, other organs such as the liver (shown here) all aid in the digestive process.*

system, which includes the lower part of the esophagus, the stomach, and the intestines. But there are other parts of the digestive system, and other important organs here as well. The spleen, pancreas, and gallbladder all help us to digest food. The kidneys and bladder, at the very bottom of the midsection, remove liquid waste from the body. And the liver is one of the body's most important organs, with many functions.

These organs are joined by a thick system of blood vessels. Throughout the body, arteries bring blood from the heart and veins take it back to the heart and lungs. In general, the major veins and arteries parallel each other, though their blood flows in the opposite direction.

The main aorta, or artery, is called simply the abdominal aorta. This thick superhighway for blood splits in two around the area of the belly button, with each branch splitting again to provide blood to the pelvic areas and the lower limbs. The inferior vena cava is the main vein in the abdominal area, running fairly close to the aorta. Its feeder system of capillaries gathers food for cells elsewhere in the body.

# CHAPTER TWO

# HOW MUCH CAN YOU STOMACH?

An easy way to understand how the digestive system works is to think of it like a factory in reverse. Factories build complex products out of many raw materials. The digestive system, however, takes complex materials and breaks them down into small pieces of raw material. It then sends these pieces along to the rest of the body to use for its energy needs and to build new tissues. The complex materials are the food we eat. The raw materials the digestive system manufactures are sugars, proteins, fats, vitamins, and other nutrients.

Digestion actually begins in the mouth. There, the teeth tear food into small bits and pass them into the esophagus, a long tube connecting the mouth to the stomach. The salivary glands add saliva as a lubricant, making it easier for the food to begin its journey. Saliva also starts breaking down starches

*While the first organ we often think of when it comes to digestion is the stomach, digestion really begins with the mouth, where teeth break apart food mechanically and saliva begins to break food down chemically.*

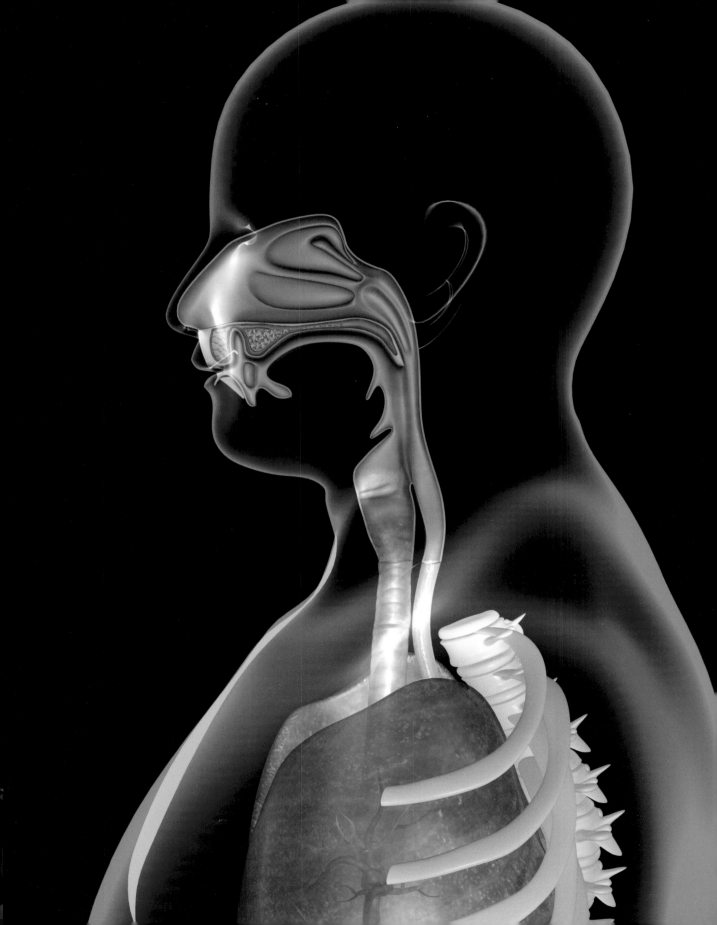

in the food. Meanwhile, the smell and taste of the food has triggered the body's digestive system, telling the stomach to get ready. Food is on the way!

Digestion can be broken into three stages. The first is preparation, where food is torn apart. This begins in the mouth and continues in the stomach. The second stage is absorption, where raw materials are absorbed into the bloodstream. This mostly takes place in the small intestine. The third stage is elimination, where unused food is collected, compacted, and passed out of the body. This takes place in the large intestine and rectum.

As it is broken down, food becomes a watery paste known as chyme. This paste is pushed by the stomach muscles through the stomach and through its gastric canal to the pylorus and then out to the intestines.

## THE HUMAN STOMACH

Shaped like a fat, angled J or backwards C, the stomach sits just beneath the liver and toward the front of the body.

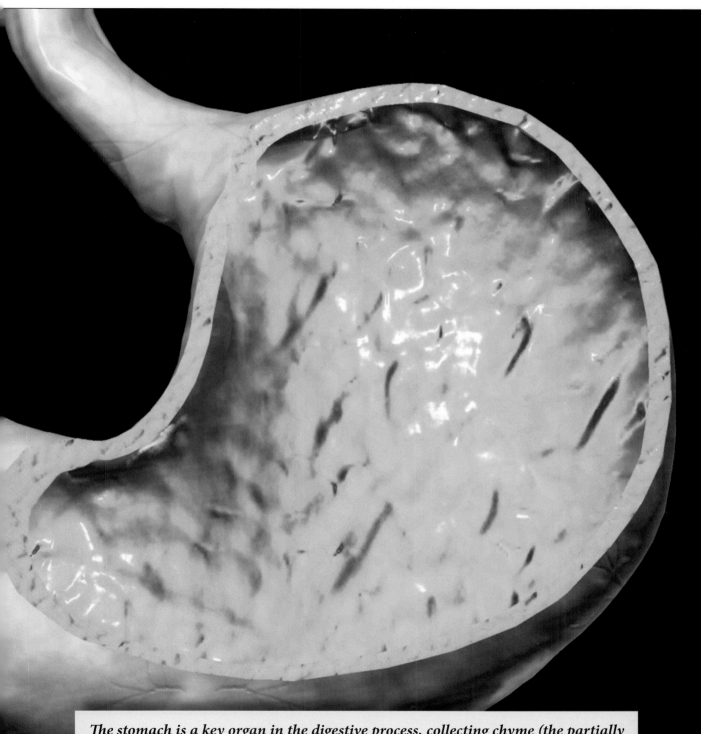

*The stomach is a key organ in the digestive process, collecting chyme (the partially broken-down food paste that is passed down by the esophagus) in order to further break food down with stomach acid.*

# A RARE PEEK INSIDE

Have you ever wondered what you would see if your body had a window? What if there were a doorway that would allow you to examine your internal organs? A freak injury in 1822 did just that to Alexis St. Martin, a fur trader on the U.S.-Canadian frontier in what is now Michigan. Shot in the side during an accident or a fight—the exact cause is unclear—St. Martin nearly died. Dr. William Beaumont managed to save him. But when St. Martin finally healed after two years, a hole remained in his side. Through the hole, Beaumont could see and touch St. Martin's lung and the inside of his stomach. The opening to the stomach had a round flap, which could be opened to observe the

*Alexis St. Martin (1800–1882) was a Canadian trapper who—following an injury at close range from a shotgun—lived with a permanent opening in the side of his stomach. Dr. William Beaumont made use of St. Martin's unique injury to truly study the human stomach in 3D!*

inside. When St. Martin was better, Beaumont conducted a number of experiments. Eventually he published a book about what he had learned.

St. Martin lived until 1880. He often spoke at medical societies, showing doctors the inside of his stomach.

When empty, a typical adult stomach is relatively small. The hollow interior might have space for only about 50 milliliters or 1.7 fluid ounces, barely a mouthful of soda. As a person eats, the stomach walls quickly stretch. The volume can increase to two or three liters, roughly three-fourths of a gallon (2.8liters) of undigested food, chyme, and gastric acid. The stomach has two basic jobs: to hold food and break it into smaller bits for digestion and absorption.

## STOMACH MUSCLES

The pinkish white exterior of the stomach covers a layer of muscles. These muscles are very active during digestion. Three layers—the outer longitudinal, the middle circular, and the inner oblique—work like giant compressors. They grind food by contracting and expanding. Together they wring the stomach and its contents like one might a thick, wet rag.

The longitudinal muscles run from the esophagus to the pyloric sphincter like the longitudinal lines on a globe. The circular muscles run around the stomach like the equator around the globe. The oblique muscles look like sinewy fibers stretching from the top, or dome, of the fundus downward.

## SECTIONS OF THE STOMACH

The stomach is divided into four different sections. From top to bottom, these are the cardia (or cardiac zone), the fundus, the body (or corpus), and the pylorus (or the pyloric part of the stomach).

The cardia includes the opening to the esophagus. A zigzag line around the interior known as the Z line marks the barrier between the two organs. Ordinarily, stomach acid is not

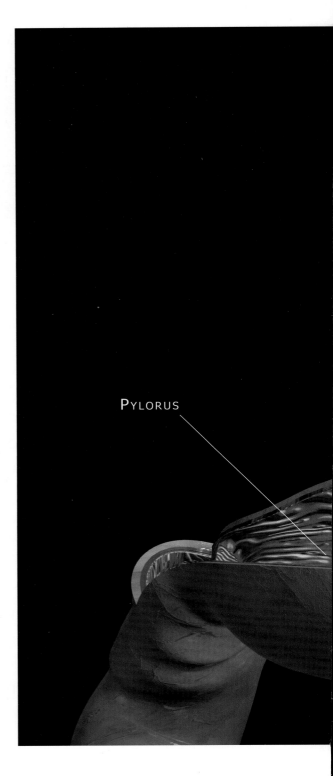

PYLORUS

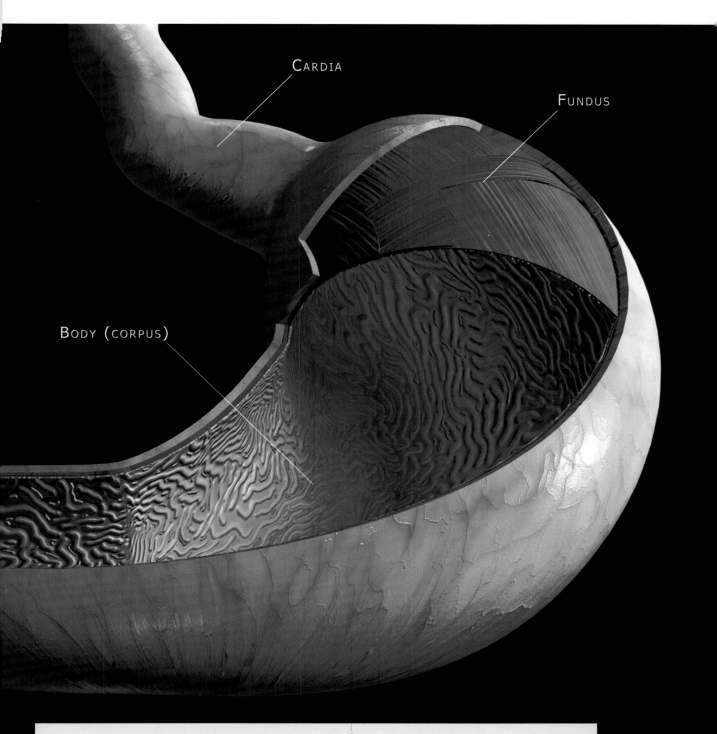

CARDIA

FUNDUS

BODY (CORPUS)

*There are four sections of the human stomach: the cardia, the fundus, the corpus, and the pylorus. Food moves through each section before being passed on to the small intestine.*

allowed past this barrier. A powerful ring of muscles called a sphincter works like a gatekeeper here. Sometimes, however, acid manages to sneak past. When that happens, the acid irritates the esophagus. We commonly call this heartburn.

The fundus is located at the top of the stomach. Shaped like a dome, it expands greatly during and immediately after a meal. It's like a reception room for food, where what we eat waits until there's room in the rest of the system.

Doctors call the main portion of the stomach the corpus, a Latin word that means "body." This part also expands and contracts. Gastric pits line the fundus and corpus. These pits are tiny holes where the stomach juices are produced.

The fourth part of the stomach looks like a large funnel at the end of the stomach. This is called the pylorus, and it curves upward toward the duodenum, the entry to the small intestine. The point between these two organs is called the pyloric opening. Muscles on the exterior of the stomach work to allow food past the opening once the stomach is done with it. This muscle door is called the pyloric sphincter.

## BURN, BABY, BURN: STOMACH ACID

The lining of the stomach is covered with mucus cells that protect it from gastric juice, which is mostly hydrochloric acid. Other cells have special jobs as well. Some help to produce the acid. Others can absorb nutrients easily.

The folds of the stomach are called rugae or gastric folds. Here the gastric juices break down the food with their powerful acid. Pepsin in the juice also goes to work. An enzyme that

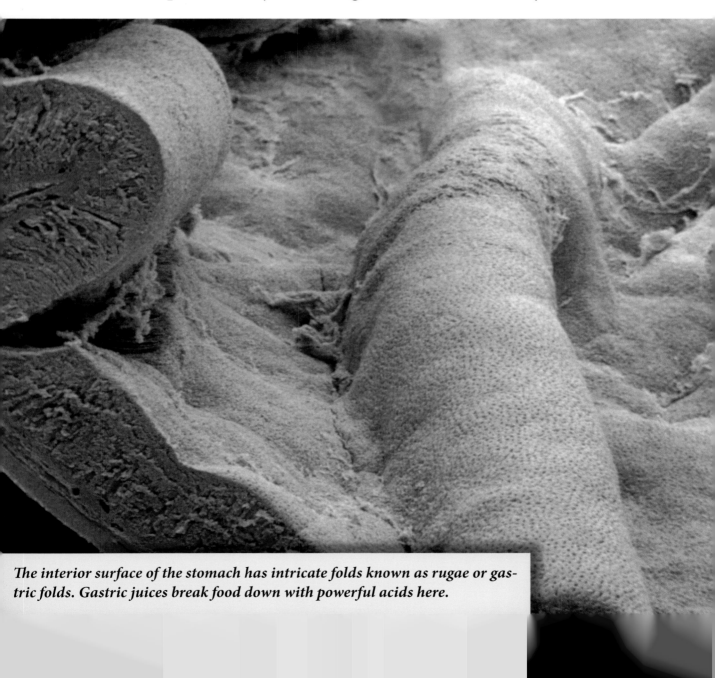

*The interior surface of the stomach has intricate folds known as rugae or gastric folds. Gastric juices break food down with powerful acids here.*

assists chemical reactions, pepsin breaks proteins down into peptides. Peptides form the building blocks of many cells and tissues. Without them, a person can't grow or even survive.

Besides breaking down food, hydrochloric acid kills bacteria that might harm the stomach and the rest of the body. The body has several other defenses against germs that enter through the digestive tract. Lymph follicles, or nodules, lie near the stomach lining. These can target invading organisms like bacteria with white blood cells. The lymph system can stamp out a disease here before it gets a chance to spread.

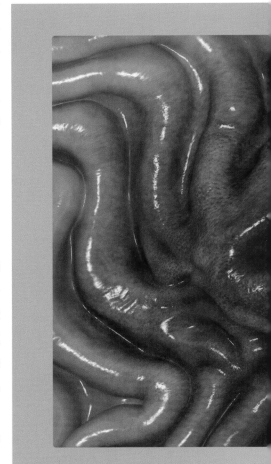

## STOMACH ILLNESSES

Often when we are sick, we vomit. A series of muscle contractions force the esophageal sphincter open and compress the stomach, sending its contents upward through the esophagus and mouth. At the same time, air openings are closed, protecting our lungs.

Usually, the body uses this system to help protect itself from poisonous food. Vomiting can be caused by irritation anywhere in the gastrointestinal tract, not just the stomach.

Ulcers are a more serious stomach problem. Because of the acid in the gastric juices, the interior of the stomach is a very caustic environment. Once in a while, stomach acid burns through the protective mucus cells and attacks the stomach wall. This can create an ulcer, an open sore that causes pain and disrupts

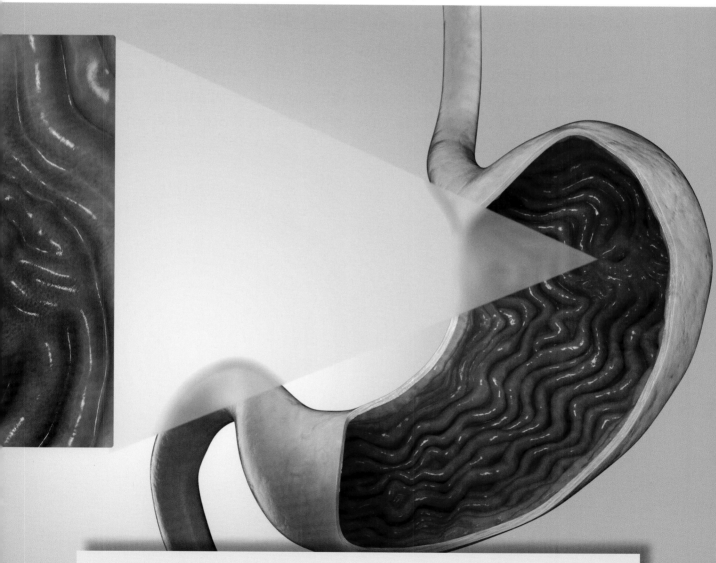

*The stomach lining has mucus cells that protect the organ's wall from the acid it contains. When the acid burns a hole through that mucus, a painful ulcer develops, as shown here.*

digestion. Scientists have worked for many years to discover why ulcers start. Besides an overproduction of acid, genetic factors and bacteria may help induce them. Special drugs such as Tagament and Ranitidine have been used to lower stomach acid and treat ulcers.

Stomach cancer can begin with symptoms that mimic ulcers. Like other cancers, cancer cells in the stomach stop following their normal blueprint for reproducing. They reproduce uncontrollably, crowding out healthy cells and disrupting vital functions. Stomach cancer is primarily treated by surgery. It is relatively rare in the United States when compared to lung cancer.

# CHAPTER THREE

# I'VE GOT A GUT FEELING

Have you ever heard the expression, "I have a gut feeling about this"? What we're really talking about when we mention the gut is our intestines. By far the largest organs of the abdomen and the longest in the entire body, the intestines are folded within the midsection like pieces of a complicated puzzle. If they were laid out in a straight line, they would stretch the length of a school bus.

Sometimes simply called the intestine, the small intestine lies below the stomach in the pit of the midsection. Its many folds eventually connect to the large intestine, or colon. The large intestine forms a thick, overturned U on the left side of the small intestine, connecting from the small intestine to the rectum.

## OUR SMALL INTESTINES

The small intestine looks like a miniature fire hose folded around the midsection of the body. This tube runs about 25 feet (8 meters) in length, yet it is only about an inch (2.5 centimeters) wide. There are three main parts. The duodenum lies next to the stomach and is the beginning of the organ. It extends about 12 inches (30 cm). Its name comes from the Latin word for twelve, *duodecim*.

The middle of the small intestine is called the jejunum. It runs about 10 feet (3 m). The ileum is the longest part of the intestine. It connects with the colon or large intestine.

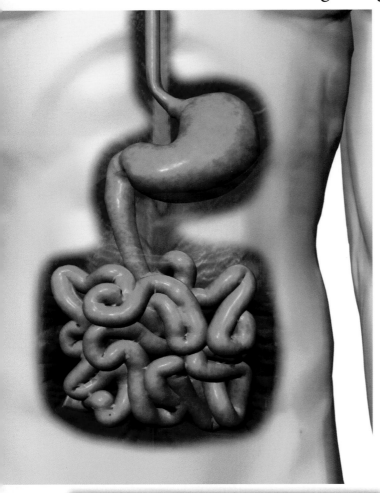

*After food has been sufficiently broken down in the stomach, it passes through the pyloric opening into the small intestine. This 25-foot (8 m) organ is tightly folded within the body's midsection.*

## SPEED IT UP WITH ENZYMES

In the duodenum, food is mixed with an alkaline fluid from the pancreas. This neutralizes the stomach acid. Then enzymes help to further break down the food.

Enzymes in the small intestine do much of the work of breaking down

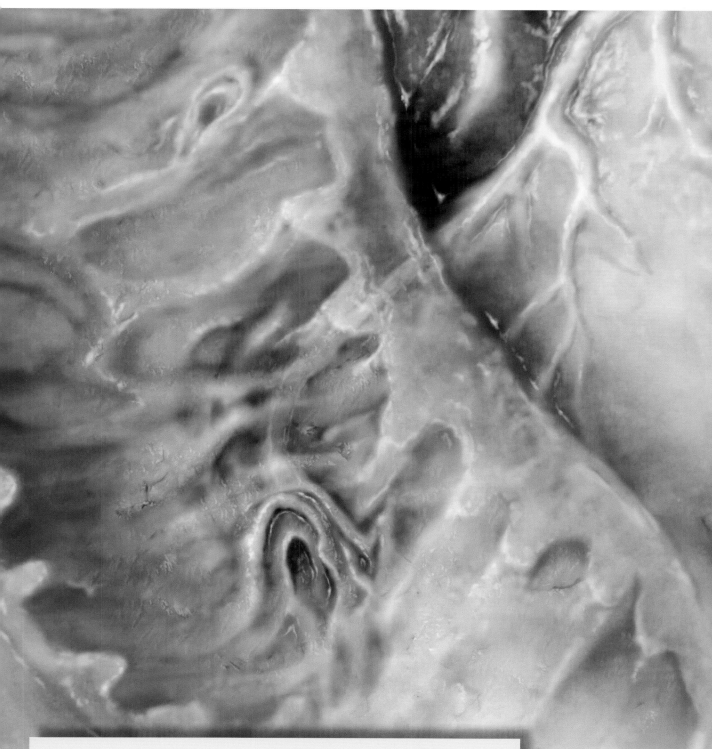

*Shown here are the common bile duct and the pancreatic duct. Enzymes (produced in the pancreas and elsewhere) and bile help further break down chyme in the small intestine.*

chyme. Enzymes are catalysts that assist chemical reactions but are not changed by them. They are large protein molecules. While in many cases chemical reactions would take place without them, enzymes help speed up the process.

A digestive enzyme called salivary amylase is injected into food in the mouth. Two more enzymes are added in the stomach, pepsin and rennin. Among the enzymes working on chyme in the small intestine are trypsin and chymotrypsin, which are both produced in the pancreas. Aminopeptidase and dipeptidase are produced in the wall of the intestine and are also vital for digesting proteins.

Complex carbohydrates are broken down with the help of pancreatic amylase, which is similar to the amylase produced by the saliva glands in the mouth. Produced in the pancreas, this enzyme does its work in the small intestines. Sugars are broken down further with the help of maltase, sucrase, and lactase, all produced in the small intestine.

Bile from the gallbladder arrives in the intestine, where it breaks fat into small droplets. Then another enzyme from the pancreas called lipase breaks the fat down further.

# OUR INTESTINAL WALLS

The breakdown and absorption of nutrients takes place on the walls of the intestines, called the intestinal mucosa. This interior surface contains ridges or folds that look a little like a corrugated drainpipe. Called epithelial folds, each fold contains billions of villi, which look like fingers extending upward, and each villus has cells with their own projections, called microvilli. This combination of folds and fingers make the intestine's surface area massive. In fact, it's roughly two hundred times as large as the surface area of the skin. Tiny blood vessels run very close to these cells to bring oxygen and ferry away nutrients.

## YOU FEEL WHAT YOU EAT

Do you think with your gut? A complex system of nerves lines the intestine, helping regulate its function. In the early 1960s, Dr. Michael Gershon began studying these nerves, called the enteric nervous system. He discovered that they create an enormous amount of serotonin. In the brain, serotonin helps us to do things like learn and rest. Gershon and others discovered other brain-like chemicals in the intestine as well.

Dr. Gershon realized that the nerve system in the intestine is like a second brain. It analyzes and reacts to different situations. It sends out chemical messages to the rest of the body. And it may affect our general mood. While the enteric nervous system can't rival the brain for thinking, scientists believe further study may reveal many clues about our overall well-being. The old saying, "You are what you eat" may have to be revised to "You feel what you eat."

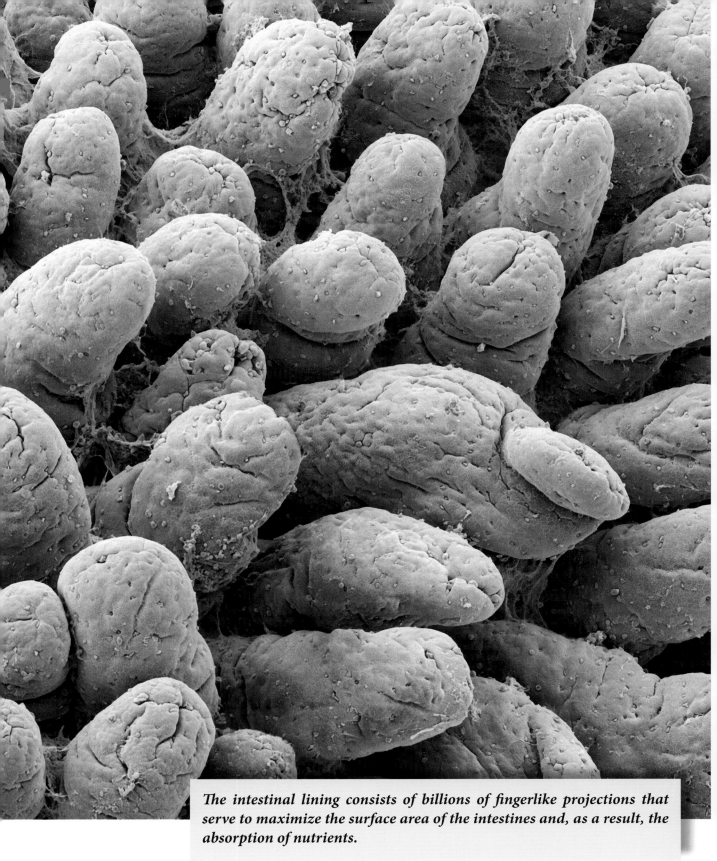

*The intestinal lining consists of billions of fingerlike projections that serve to maximize the surface area of the intestines and, as a result, the absorption of nutrients.*

# OUR COLONS

The colon rises like an upside-down box across the inside of the midsection. It climbs on your right side to about the bottom of the stomach, crosses the body, then descends down your left side before bending back to the rectum. Doctors describe the main parts of the colon simply, the ascending colon on the right, the transverse colon across, the descending colon on the left. The descending colon leads to the sigmoid colon, which connects to the rectum. ("Transverse" is a fancy way of saying "across," which describes how the colon runs across the body. "Sigmoid" comes from a Greek word meaning "S-shaped" or "curved.")

From the outside, the colon looks like a series of thick hoops or short tunnels connected together. The word "colon" comes from a Greek word for "colonnade," a series of columns. The rings are formed by the bands of muscles that expand and contract as food is passed through.

Unlike the small intestine, the colon mostly absorbs water, not nutrients. As food passes through the large intestine, it becomes drier and drier. The end result is feces.

The large intestine connects to the small intestine at the bottom of the ascending colon. The large chamber near this opening is called the cecum. It can expand and contract as food is received and then passed along. At the very bottom of the cecum, generally below the connection to the small intestine, is the appendix. This small, fingerlike projection positions itself differently in different people. The appendix does not seem to have a function in

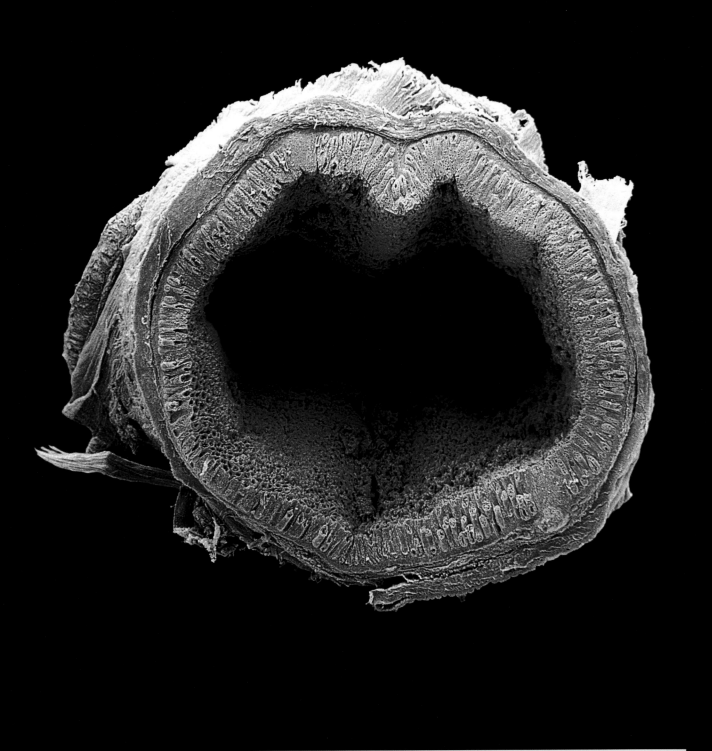

*This 3D rendering shows a transverse (or cross) view of the colon. The muscles of the colon contract in order to push food through the body until it is ultimately dispelled.*

digestion. It can, however, become inflamed or infected. In some cases, this can cause the appendix to rupture. This causes severe pain. Doctors must remove a ruptured appendix and fight the infection, or a person could die.

Food is moved through the intestines as well as the rest of the digestive system by a series of muscle contractions called peristalsis. At each point along the way, from esophagus to rectum, the arrival of food stretches the inner layer of the organ. This pushes on a layer of nerves, which in turn cause the muscles behind the food to contract. The chain reaction continues as the muscles in front of the food relax, clearing the way for the food to move forward.

Food travels through the digestive tract at a slow pace. It can take twenty-four, forty-eight, and even seventy-two hours for it to go from mouth to rectum. Usually, it stays in the large intestine the longest, with an average time of about fourteen hours. Someone who is constipated, however, may have feces remain in the colon for far longer. This condition has many causes, including a diet that doesn't have enough fiber or water. Disease can also cause constipation.

# BACTERIA & ALLERGIES

Single-cell organisms called bacteria exist everywhere in the world. Many are present in the food we eat. Unfortunately, some can cause disease and death.

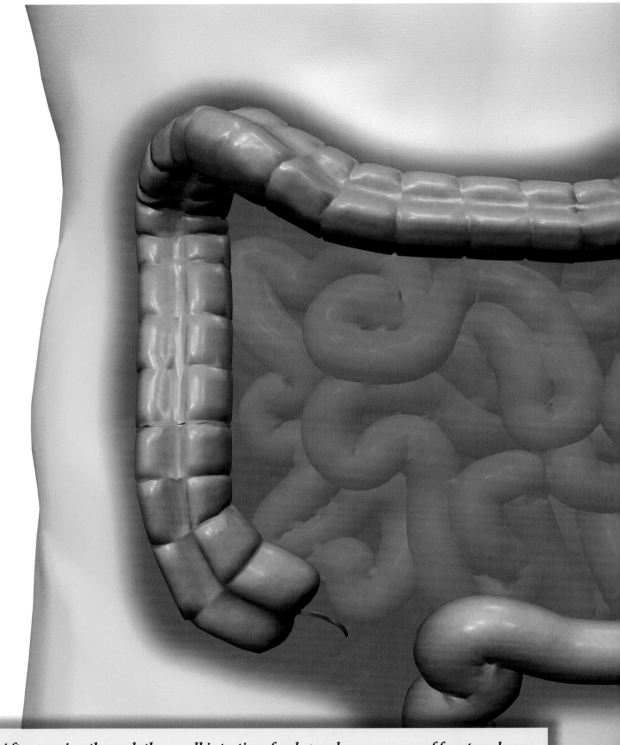

*After passing through the small intestine, food spends an average of fourteen hours in the large intestine. From start to finish, the whole digestive process can take up to seventy-two hours!*

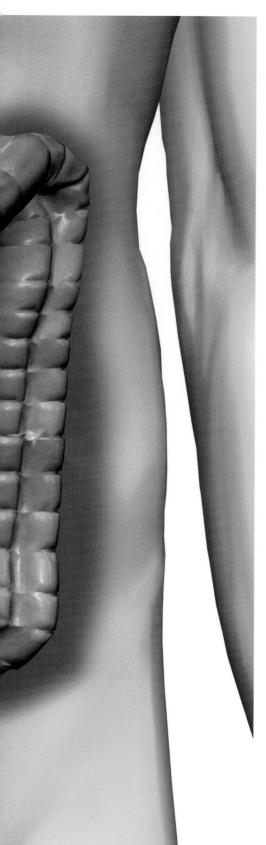

The stomach's acid bath kills much of the bacteria contained in food. Much of the rest ends up in the intestines, where harmful bacteria are attacked by the body's immune system. Microfold cells attract bacteria to lymphocytes, special cells where antibodies are made. The lymphocytes create antibodies, which then attack the bacteria.

In some people, the system malfunctions and the body reacts to the food itself as if it were enemy bacteria. The result is a food allergy. In most cases the reaction is mild, but severe allergies can cause death.

# CHAPTER FOUR

# OTHER ORGANS THAT AID DIGESTION

In addition to the stomach and the intestines, there are several other organs in the body's midsection, and all have important jobs in the digestion process. The liver, gallbladder, and pancreas manufacture chemicals important to the digestive process. The spleen and kidneys act like filters for the body, purifying it and helping to regulate the amount of water and nutrients it retains.

## OUR LIVER: A MASTER MULTITASKER

The liver is the largest gland in the body. It is also rather heavy for its size. In an adult, it accounts for about a fortieth of the body's whole weight. In a 200-pound (91 kilogram) man, it could weigh as much as five pounds (2 kg).

A rounded, upside-down triangle, the liver sits over the stomach. It has two lobes, or parts. The largest of these is on the right side of the body. The liver lies behind the rib cage and diaphragm, which help to protect it. The outside of the liver is smooth. It is brownish in color. The two lobes are joined on the outside by a ligament. Each lobe can work without the other.

The liver has several functions. It makes bile, which is necessary for digestion. Bile looks like a yellowish-green liquid. If

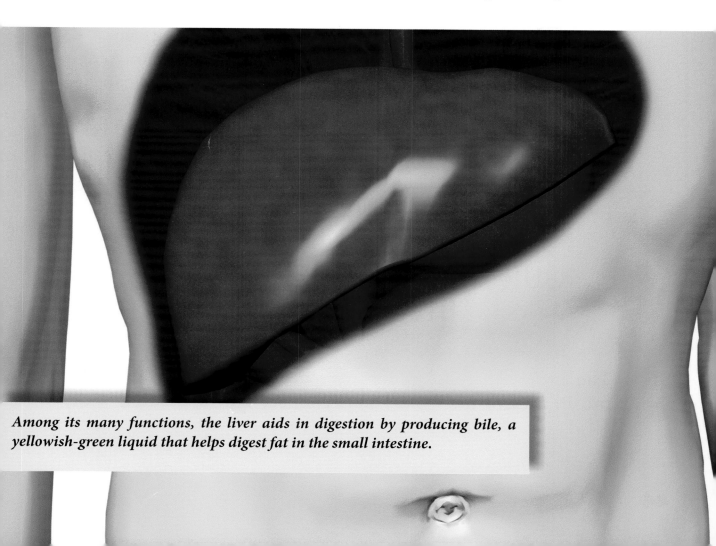

*Among its many functions, the liver aids in digestion by producing bile, a yellowish-green liquid that helps digest fat in the small intestine.*

you could taste it, it would seem extremely bitter. Bile is alkaline, or the opposite of acidic. The liver passes the bile to the gallbladder, which then dispenses it to the small intestine. Bile helps the body digest fat by emulsifying it or breaking it into small bits.

The liver also makes about a quarter of the body's lymph cells, which are used to fight disease and infection. New lymph cells enter the lymph system through lymphatic vessels, which are part of the outer layer of the organ.

The liver also helps to filter toxic materials from the blood, converting them to safer substances. Ammonia, for example, is converted to urea, which becomes urine in the kidneys. Liver cells change sugar to glycogen and help store fat and vitamins. They also synthesize blood proteins and substances such as clotting factors.

The liver cells do their work by passing blood along columns of cells that fan out from veins. This network can be easily damaged. One way is by drinking a lot of alcohol, which can cause fibers to form in the organ. These block blood vessels and disrupt the cellular architecture, preventing the cells from working right. This disease can also be caused by very poor nutrition. It is called cirrhosis.

# OUR GALLBLADDERS: WHERE BILE BACKS UP

The gallbladder looks like a green baseball tucked into the brown mitt of the liver. Ducts connect the gallbladder with

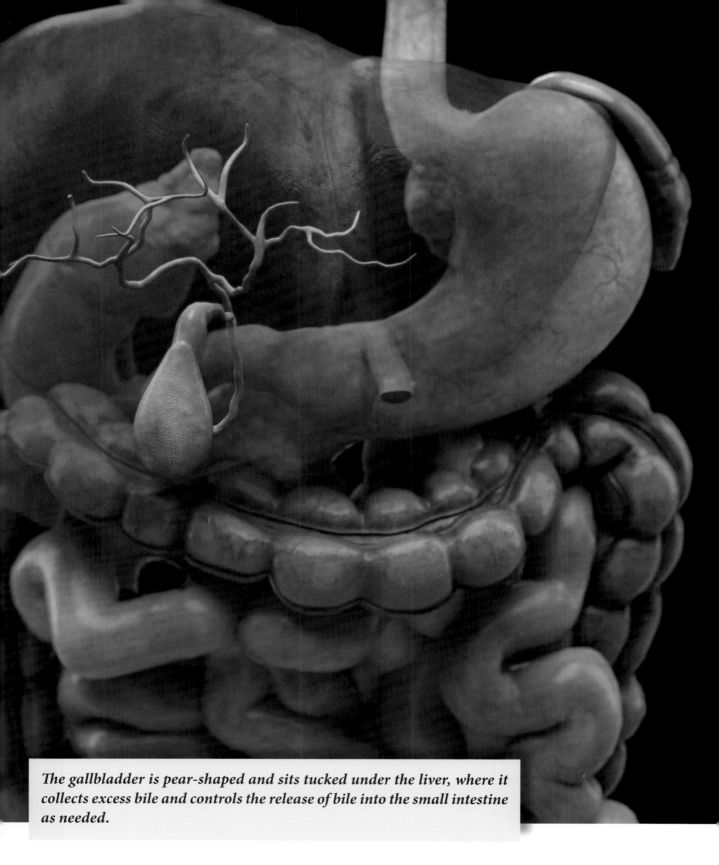

*The gallbladder is pear-shaped and sits tucked under the liver, where it collects excess bile and controls the release of bile into the small intestine as needed.*

the liver and the duodenum. These ducts work like the ducts or plumbing in a house. Bile from the liver flows down the hepatic ducts to the bile duct. A sphincter or valve at the intestine closes the connection so that the bile backs into the gallbladder. Like a thermostat, the valve opens when bile is needed, sending the liquid in from its reservoir like hot water into a radiator.

# OUR PANCREASES: IT'S ENZYME TIME

The pancreas looks a bit like an upside-down tobacco pipe, lying across the back of the abdomen. It is behind the stomach and next to the duodenum. Part of the endocrine system, the pancreas creates a variety of hormones important to the body. Insulin is probably the best known. When the pancreas doesn't produce enough of it, a person can develop diabetes, which causes high sugar levels in the blood and disrupts the body's metabolism. The pancreas also produces glucagon, another endocrine secretion that helps the body regulate itself. These hormones enter the bloodstream through vessels that extend through the organ.

The pancreas plays an important role in digestion by making pancreatic juice. This enters the duodenum through the main and accessory pancreatic ducts at the

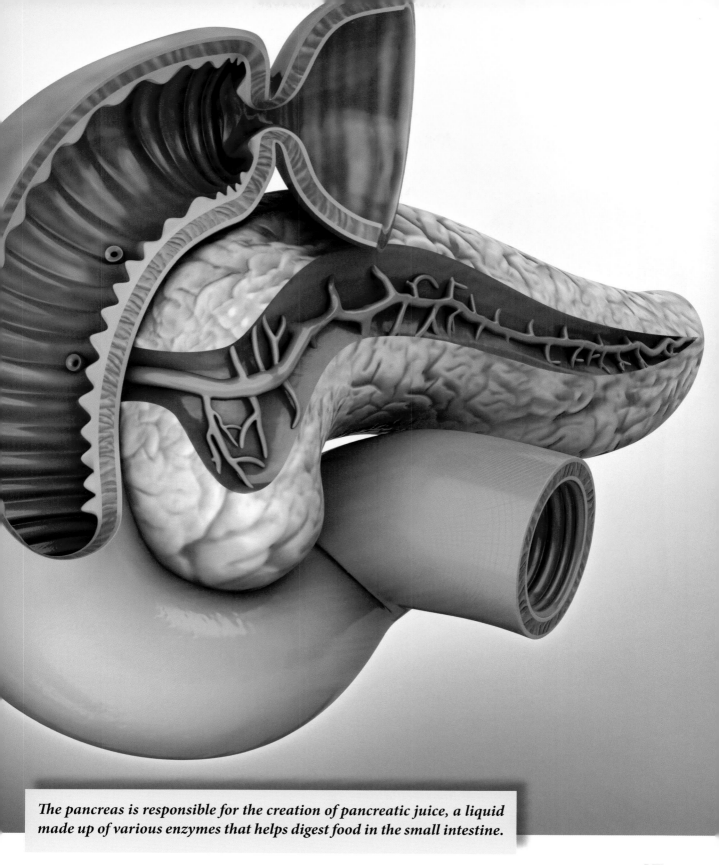

*The pancreas is responsible for the creation of pancreatic juice, a liquid made up of various enzymes that helps digest food in the small intestine.*

thick part or head of the pancreas. This juice helps break down food in the small intestine.

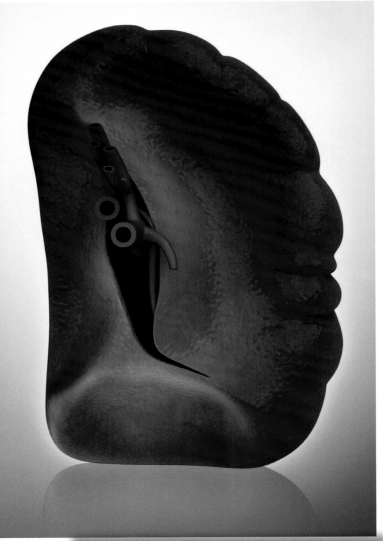

*Our spleens play important roles in fighting infections in our bodies. Blood flows into the spleen, where foreign objects are filtered out of the blood before it flows back into the circulatory system.*

# OUR SPLEENS: THE BLOOD'S FILTER

When someone yells angrily, we sometimes say that they are "venting their spleen." This metaphor refers to an ancient belief that the spleen stored vapors responsible for anger. Today, we know that's not true. The spleen's role is much more complex.

The outside of the spleen looks purplish. It is located on the left side of the body, behind the stomach. While the size and specific shape of the spleen varies from person to person, you can get a good idea of the organ's appearance by clenching your fist. Part of the lymph system, the spleen protects the body against infection. Its job is to filter foreign substances and worn-out components from the blood. It's also a reservoir, an emergency holding tank for serious bleeding.

Blood flows into the spleen from the splenic artery and through a network of small blood vessels. The spleen filters the blood, returning it to the circulatory system through the splenic vein.

# OUR KIDNEYS AND URINARY TRACTS

As it is digested, food passes through the stomach and intestines and is eventually released through the rectum as feces. Individual cells of the body expel their own waste products into the bloodstream.

These wastes, along with excess water and salts, flow through the blood to the kidneys. Shaped like large beans, the kidneys lie toward the back at the bottom of the abdomen just above the hips. The lower two rungs of the rib cage protect most of the kidneys.

The kidneys are like large filters, processing the blood that arrives from the aorta through a number of renal arteries. ("Renal" comes from the Latin word for kidney.) About 1.3 liters (44 ounces) of blood, or about the amount in a medium-sized soda bottle, flow through the kidneys each minute. In an adult, 170 liters (45 gallons) of water and liquid waste can be expelled by the kidneys in an average day.

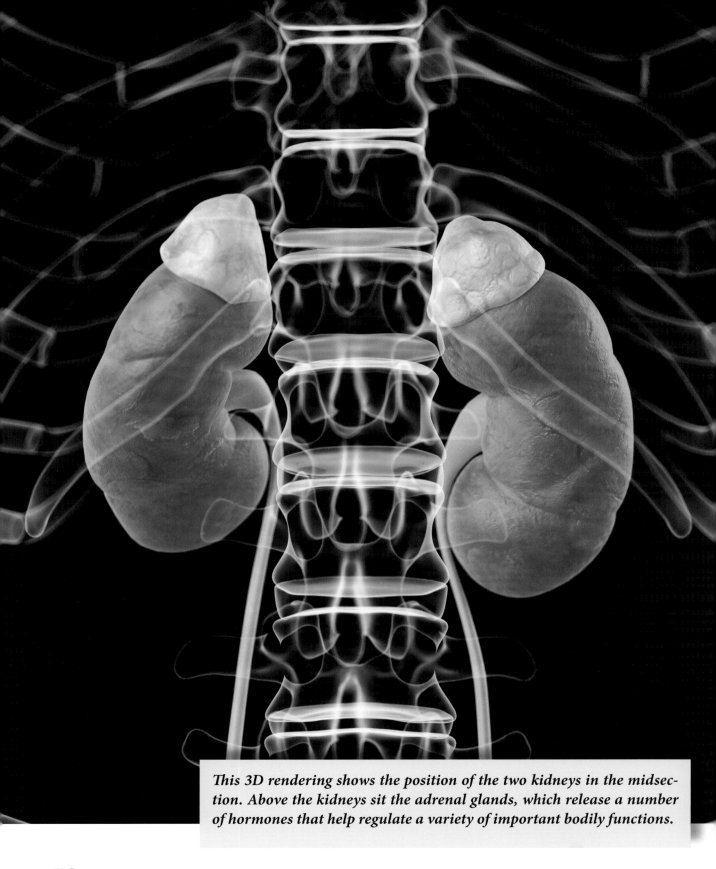

*This 3D rendering shows the position of the two kidneys in the midsection. Above the kidneys sit the adrenal glands, which release a number of hormones that help regulate a variety of important bodily functions.*

The liquid filtered out from the blood drains as urine. It flows down the ureters from each kidney to the bladder in the pelvis. The ureters are more than simply tubes. They reabsorb parts of the urine, mix it with their own secretions, and return it to the body for different functions. The rest reaches the bladder, where it collects and is then expelled.

## GET THAT ADRENALINE PUMPING!

If you've ever needed a burst of energy during a race, you called on your adrenal glands. These glands lie at the top of each kidney, next to the lower part of the diaphragm. They are also called suprarenal glands because they're on top (supra) of the kidneys, or renal

*Similar to how our digestive tract expels solid waste from the body, the kidneys filter out the waste products that cells release into our blood so it may be expelled. This liquid waste becomes urine.*

organs. Adrenaline is only one of the many hormones these glands produce. Also called epinephrine, adrenaline is joined by norepinephrine to increase heart rate and blood pressure when exercising hard or when the body must be alert. Corticosteroids and androgens cause the kidneys and other organs to retain sodium and water during stress, which increases blood pressure.

With their different hormones, the glands help to regulate a variety of bodily functions, especially during times of stress or panic.

Overall, the body's midsection might be compared to a small factory. The complex process of digestion takes place there. Other vital functions are controlled or influenced from the organs housed there. It may be called the stomach in everyday conversation, but it is much more than one digestive organ.

# GLOSSARY

**ARTERY**  A major blood vessel that carries blood from the heart to other organs of the body.

**CAPILLARY**  A small blood vessel that connects with an artery or vein.

**CHYME**  A liquid paste of food created during the early stages of digestion in the stomach.

**CONSTIPATION**  Retaining feces in the colon longer than normal. Elimination of feces varies greatly from person to person and can range from twelve to seventy-two hours after eating.

**DIGESTION**  The process of turning food into usable raw materials for cells.

**ENDOCRINE SYSTEM**  Those body systems that manufacture hormones to regulate the body's function. Major endocrine glands include the pancreas and the suprarenal glands. Other glands include the pineal gland, the hypothalamic nuclei, the pituitary, the thyroid, and the parathyroids. The male testes and the female ovaries are also part of the system.

**ENZYME**  A special protein that acts as a catalyst in the body. Catalysts are not changed by chemical reactions but are able to speed them up.

**HEARTBURN**  A burning feeling in the middle of the chest. Usually, this is caused by stomach acid leaking upward into the esophagus. It does not actually involve the heart.

**HORMONE** A chemical substance produced by the body's endocrine glands. A hormone can have a short-term effect, such as helping you to run from a scary situation. It can also have a long-term effect, such as helping to increase muscle growth.

**MUCUS** A special lining that protects the stomach from gastric acid.

**PEPSIN** An enzyme that breaks proteins down into peptides in the stomach.

**RUGAE** The folds in the interior part of the stomach.

**ULCERS** Holes in the stomach or other parts of the digestive system. Quite painful, they disrupt digestion and can be deadly if not treated.

**VEIN** A major blood vessel that carries blood back to the heart.

**VITAMINS** A wide range of organic chemicals necessary in small amounts for bodily functions.

**VOMITING** The emptying of the stomach contents through the esophagus.

# FOR MORE INFORMATION

American Gastroenterological Association (AGA)

4930 Del Ray Avenue

Bethesda, MD 20814

(301) 654-2055

Website: http://www.gastro.org

Since its founding in 1897, the AGA has grown to be a worldwide, trusted resource in the science and practice of gastroenterology. It specializes in the research of and the development of treatments for digestive diseases.

Canadian Association of Gastroenterology (CAG)

#224, 1540 Cornwall Road

Oakville, ON L6J 7W5

Canada

(888) 780-0007

Website: http://www.cag-acg.org

Since 1962, the CAG has been at the forefront of the study of the digestive tract and the promotion of digestive health in Canada. Its membership includes physicians, pediatricians, radiologists, and surgeons committed to research, education, and patient care.

Center for Gastrointestinal Biology and Disease (CGIBD)

CB #7555

Bioinformatics Building

130 Mason Farm Road

Chapel Hill, NC 27599

(919) 966-1757

Website: http://www.med.unc.edu/cgibd

The CGIBD is a collaborative research center run by the University of North Carolina–Chapel Hill and North Carolina State University to promote and improve academic research into digestion and gastrointestinal disorders.

Crohn's and Colitis Foundation of America (CCFA)

733 Third Avenue, Suite 510

New York, NY 10017

(800) 932-2423

Website: http://www.ccfa.org

The CCFA is a nonprofit organization dedicated to researching and curing Crohn's disease and ulcerative colitis through the carrying out and publication of research on both diseases.

Digestive Disease National Coalition (DDNC)

507 Capitol Court, NE, Suite 200

Washington, DC 20002

(202) 544-7497

Website: http://www.ddnc.org

The DDNC advocates for professional societies dedicated to the study and curing of digestive diseases. To that end, it works to improve public policy and expand public awareness on digestive health.

National Museum of Health and Medicine (NMHM)

2500 Linden Lane

Silver Spring, MD 20910

(301) 319-3300

Website: http://www.medicalmuseum.mil

Established during the American Civil War, the NMHM promotes the study and display of all things anatomical, with a special focus on pathology and infectious diseases.

North American Society for Pediatric Gastroenterology, Hepatology and Nutrition (NASPGHAN)

P.O. Box 6

Flourtown, PA 19031

(215) 233-0808

Website: http://www.naspghan.org

The NASPGHAN is an association of more than 1,800 pediatric gastroenterologists committed to disseminating research and information on gastrointestinal and liver health in children.

World Gastroenterology Organisation (WGO)

555 East Wells Street, Suite 1100

Milwaukee, WI 53202

(414) 918-9798

Website: http://www.worldgastroenterology.org

Consisting of more than 50,000 members worldwide, the WGO is one of the largest federations promoting educational initiatives on digestive health globally. It operates training centers and outreach programs to spread awareness of high-quality and accessible gastroenterological education.

# WEBSITES

Because of the changing nature of Internet links, Rosen Publishing has developed an online list of websites related to the subject of this book. This site is updated regularly. Please use this link to access this list:

http://www.rosenlinks.com/HB3D/Stom

# FOR FURTHER READING

Allman, Toney. *Colon Cancer.* San Diego, CA: Lucent Books, 2012.

Capaccio, George. *Digestive Disorders* (Health Alert). New York, NY: Benchmark Books, 2010.

Gillard, Arthur. *Food Allergies* (Perspectives on Diseases and Disorders). San Diego, CA: Greenhaven Press, 2014.

Gold, Susan Dudley. *Learning About the Digestive and Excretory Systems.* Berkeley Heights, NJ: Enslow Publishers, 2012.

Hand, Carol. *Living with Food Allergies* (Living with Health Challenges). Edina, MN: Abdo Publishing, 2012.

Hillstrom, Kevin. *Food Allergies* (Nutrition and Health). San Diego, CA: Lucent Books, 2012.

Juettner, Bonnie. *Diet and Disease* (Nutrition and Health). San Diego, CA: Lucent Books, 2011.

Levy, Michael, John Rafferty & William L. Hosch, eds. *Human Body I* (Britannica Illustrated Science Library). Chicago, IL: Encyclopædia Britannica, 2009.

Levy, Michael, John Rafferty & William L. Hosch, eds. *Human Body II* (Britannica Illustrated Science Library). Chicago, IL: Encyclopædia Britannica, 2009.

Parker, Steve. *Digestive and Reproductive Systems.* Mankato, MN: New Forest Press, 2010.

Parks, Peggy J. *Digestive Disorders* (Compact Research). San Diego, CA: ReferencePoint Press, 2014.

Prior, Jennifer. *The Digestive System* (TIME for Kids Nonfiction Readers). Huntington Beach, CA: Teacher Created Materials, 2012.

Rogers, Kara, ed. *The Digestive System* (The Human Body). New York, NY: Rosen Educational Publishing, 2010.

Rogers, Kara, ed. *The Kidneys and the Renal System* (The Human Body). New York, NY: Rosen Educational Publishing, 2011.

Rose, Simon. *The Digestive System* (How the Human Body Works). New York, NY: Av2 by Weigl, 2015.

Snedden, Robert. *Understanding Food and Digestion*. New York, NY: Rosen Central, 2010.

Terrazas, April Chloe. *Anatomy & Physiology, Part 2: Body Systems*. Austin, TX: Crazy Brainz, 2014.

# INDEX

# ABOUT THE AUTHOR

Maya Baden is a middle school science teacher who loves anatomy, biology, and all things science related.

James Toriello has written more than twenty books for children and young adults.

# PHOTO CREDITS

Designer: Brian Garvey; Photo Researcher: Karen Huang